D0099044

A LITTLE BIT

OF

CHAKRAS

A LITTLE BIT

OF

CHAKRAS

AN INTRODUCTION TO ENERGY HEALING

AMY LEIGH & CHAD MERCREE

STERLING ETHOS
New York

STERLING ETHOS
New York

An Imprint of Sterling Publishing Co., Inc.
1166 Avenue of the Americas
New York, NY 10036

Text © 2016 Chad Mercree and Amy Leigh Mercree
Cover © 2016 Sterling Publishing Co., Inc.

ISBN 978-1-4549-1968-1

Distributed in Canada by Sterling Publishing Co., Inc.
c/o Canadian Manda Group, 664 Annette Street
Toronto, Ontario, Canada M6S 2C8
Distributed in the United Kingdom by GMC Distribution Services
Castle Place, 166 High Street, Lewes, East Sussex, England BN7 1XU
Distributed in Australia by NewSouth Books
University of New South Wales, Sydney, NSW 2052, Australia

For information about custom editions, special sales, and premium and corporate purchases,
please contact Sterling Special Sales at 800-805-5489 or specialsales@sterlingpublishing.com.

Manufactured in the United States of America

14 16 18 20 19 17 15 13

sterlingpublishing.com

Cover design by Elizabeth Mihaltse Lindy

CONTENTS

INTRODUCTION: WHAT ARE CHAKRAS?

A Little Bit of Chakras introduces you to the mystical world of chakras, wheels of spinning energy located in specific areas of the body. Chakras are concentrations of vital life force within the body formed when lines of energy running through the body overlap and cross. For thousands of years, mystics have worked with and studied chakras and incorporated them into a wide variety of spiritual practices. Working with chakra energy in a positive way has been linked to increased lifespan; physical, mental, and emotional health; and overall personal well-being.

Conflicting information on the number, location, and purpose of chakras makes any comprehensive guide difficult to compile. This book focuses on the Western view of chakras found in contemporary New Age literature, as opposed to traditional Eastern mystical views. Therefore, we focus on seven primary chakras, running from the base of the spine to the top of the head, though we will also devote a special chapter to some of the additional chakras written about over the last two thousand years.

Each chakra is linked to organs within the body, emotional and mental attitudes, physical health or disease, colors, sounds, psychic abilities, and many other things. Some of these associations are symbolic, others based on mathematical formulas, and some on personal opinion by well-regarded spiritual practitioners. There is a widely held belief in the New Age movement that energy and consciousness are the same thing, and in this sense, chakra energy also holds aspects of our consciousness. Yogis and mystics have found many ways of working with these centers of consciousness, and we'll share some exercises and meditations to help you connect on a personal level with at least seven of your chakras.

Chakras are a part of a much larger human auric field. The aura is a dynamic field of energy that surrounds and permeates the human body. It is in constant motion like a pulsating cloud, and its quality, color, and vibrations change from moment to moment, thought to thought, feeling to feeling. Psychics believe we spiritually connect to other people, the world around us, and to the entire universe through our energy body, the aura. The physical body is simply the densest aspect of our earthly being. The aura more truly represents who we really are and the chakras are an important part of our auras because they connect our dense physical and our lighter auric fields together.

Chakras are concentrated points of energy within us, and when they are healthy, vital life energy flows through them unimpeded. When this happens, their colors are bright and clear. The opposite occurs during energetic imbalances; their colors are more dense, dark, and dull. Oftentimes when psychics "read" people they are tuning in to the quality of energy they detect within our auric fields, including our chakras. Just as medical doctors believe we store memories physically in our brains, though the exact mechanism has yet to be discovered, so psychics believe we store memories spiritually in our auric field. Psychics can "see" memories, emotional states, and past lives—really all kinds of information in our auric fields and chakras.

As you'll read in Chapter Two: The History of Chakras, the concept of chakras has been around for over two thousand years in India, and for thousands of years Chinese Taoists moved their chi, or vital life force, through various "stations" that correspond more or less to the concept of Indian chakras. Both systems used visualization to bring human awareness to these points of energy found within the body, typically during periods of meditation. Thanks to written records, we're able to see the discovery and changing perceptions about chakras and the larger energy field surrounding humans, the aura, through thousands of years of human history.

Between the dawn of Indian Upanishad philosophy and Chinese Taoist philosophy and the New Age movement of today, the concept of chakras has drastically changed. Different religions, sects within religions, philosophers, and mystics around the world described chakras differently, and there is no one consensus about what they look like or even where they're located. However, over time, ideas about chakras have brought them from an abstract visualization to a living, breathing, integral part of human consciousness. This book shares contemporary Western views about chakras being energy centers that influence physical, emotional, and spiritual healing and well-being.

A Little Bit of Chakras is laid out sequentially from one chakra to the next, moving up the body from the base of the spine to the top of the head. We recognize seven main chakras in the body, though many "minor" chakras are also recognized. Chapters Three through Nine are devoted to each of the seven chakras—root, sacral, solar plexus, heart, throat, third eye, and crown. Each chakra is associated with certain colors, organs, emotional and physical states, elements, sounds, and other things. Some people see chakras as key concepts in attaining advanced levels of spiritual development, for example, in some types of kundalini yoga. Each chakra chapter includes exercises and meditations to help you connect and work with the energy and quality of a particular energy center. Once you learn to work with the energies of each chakra, it's possible to incorporate working with them into any spiritual practice.

Chapter Ten explores the intriguing realm of additional chakras beyond the primary seven. The location, importance, shape, and function of these additional chakras vary from tradition to tradition and this book will focus on some of the more commonly recognized ones. As with the traditional seven, you can learn to connect with these additional energy centers and work with them to bring about deeper healing, wisdom, and spiritual awakening.

Thanks to the mini-New Age movement of the late 1800s and early 1900s, spiritual concepts from the East have been trickling into the West for over one hundred years. People from all walks of life and all spiritual faiths have incorporated Eastern philosophies into their lives.

We hope you enjoy *A Little Bit of Chakras*. The world of chakras has a colorful past that has contributed greatly to the spiritual, physical, emotional, and mental well-being of thousands upon thousands of spiritual seekers. We wish the same for you.

HOW TO USE THIS BOOK

WORKING WITH CHAKRAS, AND THE greater human energy field, can positively impact your health and well-being. It's also a great way to get in touch with your personal spirituality. *A Little Bit of Chakras* gets you familiar with where chakras are in the human body and how to connect with them through easy-to-follow guided meditations. If you have any concerns about meditation or energy work, please consult a physician prior to trying any of the practices contained in this book. If at any time you feel uncomfortable physically, mentally, or emotionally, please consult your doctor for advice.

Traditionally, spiritual energy work took place under the guidance of an experienced teacher. The ever-independent West is populated by many do-it-yourselfers, and if you count yourself among them, please proceed slowly, and if at any time you encounter obstacles, seek out a spiritual teacher for guidance. Over the past several thousand years, millions of people have discovered the positive health effects from kundalini yoga practice, and meditation in general, and all the practices in this book fall on the gentlest side of the meditation spectrum. However, *A Little Bit of Chakras* is just the tip of the iceberg when it comes to Hindu and New Age philosophy, and in the brief chapters ahead, we won't have the space to share a full overview of the comprehensive ancient philosophies at the root of chakra energy. This is an entertaining and educational guide that will hopefully inspire you to embark on deeper spiritual discovery.

This is an introduction to the world of chakras and learning how to work with them. You don't have to read the chapters sequentially. Pick a chakra that interests you and follow along with the meditation and exercise in that particular chapter. These meditations and exercises can be repeated as often as you like until you achieve the positive results you desire. We recommend carving out thirty to sixty minutes to complete the exercises in each chapter, and it is best to practice in a quiet, comfortable location where you won't be distracted. Wear comfortable clothing and choose a place to sit or lie down that helps your body remain relaxed throughout the entire exercise. Exercises can be done at any time of day or night, and if you fall asleep while meditating, that's okay, too. It just means you needed some rest.

At the end of *A Little Bit of Chakras* there's a list of amazing additional resources to point you in the right direction if you want to learn more about chakras from ancient times to today. Anything referenced in these pages can be found in the Bibliography section, from books and manuscripts to Web sites.

THE HISTORY OF CHAKRAS

S O WHAT ARE CHAKRAS, REALLY, AND WHY BOTHER trying to understand them? To answer that we need to understand how ancient Hindus saw the world. Chakras are part of a much larger philosophy about the composition of the universe and humanity's place in spiritual universal hierarchy. Without putting chakras in context, they can appear to be just another New Age fad, when in reality they are anything but.

The idea of chakras developed in ancient India and is part of a larger philosophy and spiritual practice called kundalini yoga. Kundalini yoga grew in popularity in ancient India at a time when the established Hindu Vedic priestly system of heavy ritual and animal sacrifices lost favor among the masses. Many people sought a more personal spiritual life and spent the best years of their lives in meditation and solitary spiritual pursuits. Mystics developed several systems of yoga and philosophy to reflect their spiritual discoveries.

Generally speaking, adherents of kundalini yoga believe the practice is especially effective during this cycle of human existence, the Kali Yuga, roughly translating to Dark Age. During this time it's believed to be exceptionally difficult to achieve enlightenment, and it's believed that confusion and materialism will continue to be obstacles to human development. Kundalini yoga methods overcome these obstacles by essentially spiritualizing the human body, creating a light body within the physical body.

Kundalini takes years to master and is a very difficult path to follow. Kundalini refers to a life force energy that lies dormant at the base of the human spine. Kundalini yoga includes practices to awaken this energy and send it up through the body toward the crown of the head before it's brought back down to the spine in a complete energetic loop. Along the way, the kundalini energy rises through several energy centers within the body. These centers are called chakras, and their number, quality, and location vary from teacher to teacher. Once chakras are awakened, it is believed their transformative effects on the human body will contribute to health, longevity, mental clarity, and so forth. So in traditional terms one can't speak of chakras without speaking about kundalini yoga.

Indian spiritual wisdom was passed on orally from teachers to students for hundreds, maybe thousands of years before being written down. The first written records of mystic Indian philosophy, which included kundalini yoga concepts as well as many other things, appeared roughly between 600 and 800 BCE, about 2,700 years ago.

Today, only about two hundred of these documents survive, and only a few of those are considered to be major works of interest. These two hundred documents are not taken together like the various books of the Bible. Each work has its own perspective, but collectively they have been compiled into a body of literature called the Upanishads.

Upanishad derives from the Sanskrit words upa ("near") and nishad ("sitting down"), and roughly translates to "at the foot of the teacher." The collected works of the Upanishads were tools expounded upon by a knowledgeable teacher to their student, rather than as a standalone guidebook. The earliest Upanishads express ideas about reincarnation, karma, and enlightenment, and later Upanishads, written between the second century BCE and the second century CE, mention the concepts of chakras, mantras, and Tantric yoga.

The Upanishads mention two key spiritual forces: Brahman and Atman. Brahman is the underlying, unexpressed, causal force of reality. Brahman energy creates everything in every universe but exists outside time and space. Atman is the life force, the underlying true essence, within every living thing. Through meditation we can connect with our Atman essence. The Hindu goal of enlightenment, moksha, is to maintain a connection with Atman in such a way that we return to our Atman source and thus transcend death and reincarnation. This is possible because in truth Atman and Brahman are the same essence, and returning to Atman is returning to Brahman, beyond all our mental concepts of reality.

Atman energy flows through the human body along specific lines of energy called nadis. It's similar to the concept of energy meridians in traditional Chinese medicine. Nadis are like veins of energy that flow through living beings. In distinct places these energy lines cross one another at certain points in the body. Some of these crossings result in nadi lines folding and twisting many times over to form knots of energy. These knots are chakras.

Meditation calmed the mind, body, and emotions and allowed mystics to feel the Atman vital force flow through them. Nadi energy flows via prana, the breath, through the body in a complex flow pattern, but all of this energy converges at the heart, believed to be the center of consciousness. Some texts describe seventy-two thousand nadi lines converging on the heart center; others mention several hundred thousand.

Some yogic texts describe chakras as visualization tools used by Tantric yogis on their quest for spiritual awakening, in which case chakras were not necessarily believed to be independent of their visualizations. The yogis created the chakras through their visualizations as a way to store spiritual energy for use during more advanced spiritual practices. Storing life force energy was believed to be a requirement to achieve enlightenment and students would spend a lifetime learning to be able to hold enough energy to enlighten. Many other yogis believe chakras exist no matter what, and have psychically seen them as living light energy.

By the second century BCE these twisted and folded bundles of nadis were recognized as distinct energy centers called chakras.

In Sanskrit, the written language of ancient India, chakra means "wheel," and described the shape the mystics saw. They were also described as petals of a flower, with some chakras having two petals and others having an infinite number. Chakras had many conflicting descriptions and this trend continues to this day. The location, color, size, quality, and purpose of chakras vary from philosophy to philosophy, mystic to mystic.

Tantric Buddhism is a Tibetan Buddhist practice that stems from Indian Tantra. They have a different view of the number, location, and makeup of chakras in the body. Other traditions, including yogas such as laya and kundalini, as well as the nineteenth-century religion of Radha Soami, to name but a few, put their own unique spin on the chakras and energetic spiritual development in the past two thousand years.

Even today in Indian philosophy there is no consensus about where the nadis flowed through the body, how many times the nadi lines twisted up to form chakra points, nor where these points could be found in the body. Early twentieth-century guru Sri Aurobindo's chakra system recognized seven chakras but their importance and meaning was unique to his teachings. But there is a universal acceptance of the importance of chakras to our physical and spiritual well-being, and over millennia, the traditional understanding of chakras and human energy fields continues to develop.

Over time, India's religious landscape continued to diversify. In the Indian subcontinent, Buddhism and Jainism emerged from the foundations of Hindu religion and philosophy. Both new religions embraced personal spiritual development and the concept of chakras, along with the mystical traditions of their ancestors, including beliefs in karma, reincarnation, and enlightenment, remained important. Eventually, many Eastern spiritual traditions made their way to the West, especially starting in the nineteenth century.

In the nineteenth and twentieth centuries, several influential authors and personalities shaped the Western view of Eastern religion and mysticism. These views have stood the test of time and were the source of the New Age movement and modern pop spirituality, and it is from these views that much of the information in this book is derived. These authors' opinions on chakras, more than any other, firmly shaped the philosophies found in New Age philosophies.

In 1875, the Theosophical Society was formed by Helena Blavatsky and several of its founding members—especially Annie Besant, Charles Leadbeater, and Henry Olcott—wrote books on metaphysical topics ranging from Ascended Masters and the seven rays to clairvoyance and magic. Blavatsky claimed some of her teachings were channeled by Ascended Masters, the Mahatmas or the Great White Brotherhood, who were living in a hidden location in Tibet. As a group, the Theosophical Society promoted ancient beliefs in the power of the number seven, and applied them to a whole host of metaphysical concepts, including chakras. In 1927, Charles Leadbeater published the book The Chakras, and in true Theosophical form, recognized seven chakras. He described them as generally multicolored and of varying degrees of complexity. This was in keeping with the yogic view of chakras. However, the locations and meaning of the seven chakras, as well as their colors, differ from the contemporary view.

Madame Blavatsky claimed to have traveled extensively in India and other places deemed remote by nineteenth-century European standards, and purported to have studied with physical and spiritual masters. Modern New Age ideas about the Ascended Masters and the magical powers of the archangels can be traced back to the teachings of the Theosophical Society. In terms of the chakras, their views on the location and significance of each chakra influences Western pop culture to this day.

The other great influence on the Western world's understanding of chakras was Sir John George Woodroffe (aka Arthur Avalon) whose groundbreaking book *The Serpent Power: The Secrets of Tantric and Shaktic Yoga*, published in 1919, introduced the West to kundalini yoga, chakras, and Tantric teachings. The Serpent Power was based on translations from two Tantric yoga texts: "Description of the Six Chakras" and "Fivefold Footstool" by Swami Purnananda from 1526 CE. In contrast to the Theosophical Society, Woodroffe's work was scholarly and very technical and is still recognized as a solid contribution to the Western understanding of Eastern traditions. Other publications appeared around this time, including "System of Chakras According to Gorakshanatha" in 1923, which lists thirty-one main chakras in an array of colors, including "smoky."

Our contemporary concept of the seven chakras corresponding to the seven colors of the rainbow can be traced to Christopher Hills, whose 1977 book *Nuclear Evolution: Discovery of the Rainbow Body* had a profound yet forgotten influence on the New Age movement. His book went into some detail about the finer points of each chakra, none of which particularly caught on with readers. But the flashy association of the seven chakras with the seven colors of the rainbow stuck.

Almost ten years later, in 1988, Barbara Ann Brennan's book *Hands of Light* took a scientific approach to chakras and introduced readers to chakras as spinning vortexes of energy that emerge at the front and back of the human body. These vortexes connect to cosmic forces, and she used this concept extensively in her healing practice. She described chakra-vortexes in many locations of the body, including hands, feet, and most joints. Both Barbara Ann Brennan and Christopher Hills' approaches to chakras appear to have been influenced by the Theosophists, and in the twenty-first century, opinions about the hows and whys of chakras continue to evolve.

In the end, the Theosophists' influence most strongly influenced the Western understanding of chakras, and almost one hundred years later their collected works quietly inspire contemporary New Age authors. Perhaps as more attention is paid to these energy centers in the human body, new ideas about their function and purpose will emerge. We all have an opportunity to develop a personal understanding about our own chakras; you may be surprised at how easy it is to feel them. With practice, you may come to see, feel, and work with these and other energy centers in your body in a transformative way. From chakras' origin as visualizations to Barbara Brennan's view of them as three-dimensional spinning vortexes of light, our ideas and beliefs about chakras has dramatically changed over the past two thousand years, and will likely continue to evolve and grow into the future.

MULADHARA—
THE ROOT
CHAKRA

I N SANSKRIT, THE WORD *MULADHARA* MEANS "ROOT support." The root chakra is located at the base of the spine. Most traditions describe it as red in color. Some people see the shades of red as bright cherry and some as a more on the maroon end of the spectrum. Part of the color perception of a chakra involves how bright and light it is—the lighter and brighter, the better. Since chakras are made of energy we want it to be clear, luminous, and not muddy or dim.

In Tantric tradition, it has four deep red petals.

Muladhara governs survival, security, and your walk in the world. This chakra is all about support. It supports the rest of your physical body because it is at the base of the spine. It relates to how supported you feel in this world materially. A healthy and clear root chakra will bring vitality to your feet and legs. The energy flowing there will be strong and rich.

When in balance, muladhara resonates security, stillness, and stability. It helps you feel safe in the world and sure that your needs will be met, especially your basic physical needs for shelter, food, water, sleep, clothing, and material comfort. Because of our urge to be stable and secure in this world, we all seek strength in the root chakra.

Gravity is this chakra's most influential force. In essence, it holds your feet to the ground gently and effortlessly. Being "grounded" is a term you may have heard that refers to the root chakra. Being grounded means that you are rooted and present in your body and on the planet.

The body and presence are critical to health and happiness. Ideally, the body feels grounded and present. This feeling stems from the security of the root chakra. Strength and balance in the root chakra paves the way for a life that is stable and secure.

EXERCISE: MEDITATION TO CONNECT WITH YOUR ROOT CHAKRA

Connecting more deeply to your root chakra will help you develop greater awareness of it and all of your chakras. It will awaken you to the spinning vortices of light within you and help you harness their power. Feeling your root chakra will enliven your being and help you feel more present in this world.

Select a quiet and calm spot where you will be undisturbed for about fifteen minutes. Get as comfortable as possible. You may sit down or lie down—simply choose a position where it is relatively unlikely you will fall asleep. If you do drift off to sleep during this practice, that is okay. It simply means your body wanted to go deeper and open up more of a healing wellspring within you and it would work best with your conscious mind out of the picture for a spell.

Close your eyes and listen to your breathing. As you listen to the air entering and leaving your mouth, begin to allow each breath to deepen and slow. Feel your body begin to relax and dip deeper into the flow of your breath and the serenity of the moment.

Now, picture the most clear, light, bright version of the color red you can imagine. Envision this color made of light rays or particles. Let this red glow into your inner sight. Stay focused on the color and allow yourself to gently merge into it more and more.

Now, place your hands on the lowest part of your abdomen or even on your buttocks. Feel your hands connect to your root chakra and see the beautiful red color you were watching in your own root chakra. Feel it pulsing there.

Now, repeat the seed mantra associated with the root chakra aloud, "Lam." Say the word as your feel your hands connected to the moving energy of the chakra within you. Repeat "Lam," and continue to sink into the awareness of your root chakra.

Repeat the mantra and this process for as long as you'd like. When you feel it is complete, bring your awareness back into the room and briskly rub your hands, feet, legs, and arms while saying, "I am here now. I am present." Make sure you feel completely back to yourself before going on with your day. Drinking water may assist in this process.

Each of your chakras is associated with one or more endocrine glands. The root chakra governs the adrenal glands. The adrenal glands are located on top of the kidneys and kick in when you experience fight-or-flight response. They pump out adrenaline in crisis situations.

A type of endocrine dysfunction that is sometimes associated with the adrenals is adrenal fatigue. This is symptomatic of misfiring and/or overactive adrenal glands. In modern life, although you are seldom in immediate physical danger, your adrenals may misunderstand emotional and mental stress and react like you are in mortal danger. A mind/body remedy for this is meditation and relaxation.

The parts of the body associated with the root chakra are the feet, legs, perineum, coccygeal plexus, rectum, and large intestine. Some potential physical signs of root chakra dysfunction include hemorrhoids; bowel issues, including constipation and diarrhea; sciatica; and knee and lower back pain.

Emotional, mental, or spiritual dysfunction in this chakra include overidentification with material possessions, hoarding supplies, being ungrounded or spacy, and excessive or irrational fear.

To promote health and vitality in these areas you can visually take in clear, bright shades of red, especially if you feel the chakra is underactive or does not have enough chi or energy flowing within it. This chakra is specifically associated with the Earth and ground, so one of the healthiest things you can do for it is to walk outside with bare feet. A close second is to be outside. Lying down in a park, meadow, or at the beach and being close to the Earth will strengthen this chakra and it may balance your adrenal glands, too.

When you think about the health of your root chakra, think about your foundation and how it is the basis of everything in your life. Imagine if your deepest beliefs and foundational thoughts and feelings were aligned with the healthiest possible energy. Imagine if your needs and personal safety and security were completely fulfilled. This is what the energy of the root chakra powers.

If the energy of your root chakra is in balance you will feel safe driving a car. You will feel supplied as far as your material needs. You will feel as if you are standing squarely and strongly on the Earth as you walk through your life. Your root chakra is a source of strength in the earthly world. Be rooted in today. Be rooted in your life. Be rooted in the world. Be here now.

EXERCISE: ACTIVITY TO CONNECT WITH YOUR ROOT CHAKRA

Your root chakra is all about being present to life and feeling grounded. Use the following meditation process frequently to help you get in touch with the roots that tether you to the planet, that nourish and sustain you. Read this aloud or quietly to yourself or record it digitally to play back if that will be easier for you. Sit or lay down for this exercise. You may do this indoors or outdoors in a safe, quiet space to relax and experience.

Place your attention on the soles of your feet. Feel roots grow out of each foot and out of your tailbone; send them into the Earth. They may combine into one large root or remain two or three separate roots. All of these variations are fine, and you do not have to know which one is happening right now.

Feel these roots growing deeper and deeper through soil and dirt, through the matrix of rock and stone, through aquifers full of water. Continue growing your roots down through the magma in the mantle of the planet. Finally grow them into the core of the Earth. Feel them sucked into the inner core of the planet. Held. Stable. Strong. Rooted.

Feel the energy and vibration of the Earth flowing up your roots and into your feet and tailbone. Feel it pulsing within you. Hear the inner heartbeat of the planet. Hear it beating like a gentle drum. Merge with this interdimensional sound.

Experience deep communion with the Earth. Feel her love for you expand into each cell in your body. All is right with you and your mother, the Earth. She has infinite strength and she shares this wellspring of stability and strength with you, her child. Thank the Earth for this huge gift.

Allow your awareness to come back into the room or area in which you are sitting or lying down. Feel whatever your body is touching—the chair, the bed, the ground. Wiggle your toes and fingers.

With your awareness fully in the moment and eyes open, feel your root(s) pulsing below you. Maintain this awareness for as long as you are able. Walk around still feeling your roots.

Place your attention on the soles of your feet. Experience what it feels like to be fully present and grounded in the moment, in the NOW.

ROOT CHAKRA AFFIRMATION

"I AM GROUNDED AND PRESENT IN MY LIFE."

4

SVADHISHTHANA —THE SACRAL CHAKRA

IN SANSKRIT, THE WORD *SVADHISHTHANA* MEANS "sweetness." The sacral chakra is located in the lower abdomen and womb. It is generally thought to be orange. Some people picture it as a clear, vivid orange, like the color of the fruit. Some picture it a bit lighter or more golden. The brighter you perceive the chakra to be, the healthier it is. We want your chakras to be luminous, clear, and full of light. This means the energy is flowing and balanced. To unblock energy in your chakras, you focus on filling them with light and letting go of any past density that you may hold there.

Tantric traditions believe that this chakra has six vermilion red petals. In this chapter, we will be working from the Western theory of chakras, where the chakra is orange.

Svadhishthana governs pleasure, desire, sexuality, sensuality, and procreation. It is all about the sweetness of life and feeling good. This chakra enlivens your world experience by engaging your senses and emotions. This is a complicated, rich, and, when in balance, rewarding chakra. A healthy and vibrant sacral chakra will help you enjoy life to the fullest. It brings vitality through pleasure and enjoyment and can be a source of great joy.

When in balance, svadhishthana gives you the ability to navigate change and the polarities of life. It also resonates pleasure, movement, emotions, sexuality, and nurturance. It helps you engage in the sensory experience of living and integrate that energy into your subtle bodies. The human urge to procreate and be close to a romantic partner is part of the dance of the sacral chakra.

Attraction of opposites is the chief force influencing svadhishthana. You can think of this as the attraction of opposites from a purely physiological sense with men and women and how the areas of the body governed by the sacral chakra are opposite in a way that can result in procreation. That is why this chakra is your creative energy center. It is where you birth what you want to manifest or share with the world.

Feeling lively and creative is critical to a happy life. Ideally, you feel vital, alive, creative, and you experience the sensory pleasures of life (not just sexual) daily. Those feelings stem from a healthy sacral chakra. Creativity and sweetness in the sacral chakra pave the way for a life of enjoyment and feeling good.

EXERCISE: MEDITATION TO CONNECT WITH YOUR SACRAL CHAKRA

A deeper connection to your sacral chakra will help you develop your consciousness by being aware of all of your chakras. It will help strengthen the energy of this chakra that can enhance your life with vitality and pleasure. Feeling the energy of your sacral chakra will help you partake of the sweetness of this world.

Choose a tranquil spot to do this meditation where you will not be distracted for about fifteen minutes. You can sit down or find a comfy spot to lie down. If you drift off to sleep during this meditation, it is okay. This will only happen if you are very sleepy or if your body wants to go deeper with the healing and clearing you are experiencing and it wants to get your conscious mind out of the mix for a few minutes.

Relax and feel the interface of your skin with your clothing and the chair or couch beneath you. Notice any air on your bare skin. Does it feel cool, warm, comforting? Now start to bring your attention to the air you are breathing in and out. Notice it as it moves through your mouth and windpipe. Does is feel cool, breezy? Continue watching your breath. Sink deeper into the sound of its movement. With each breath, let your muscles relax more and feel your body sink into the chair or couch. Let each exhalation release more and more tension.

Now, envision a gorgeous, bright, vibrant orange. Picture this made of particles or rays of light, your choice. Watch this orange radiate on the screen of your inner sight. Focus on the color and let yourself be drawn into it. Merge with it by focusing your attention on it.

Next, place your hands on your lower abdomen. Feel your hands connect with your sacral chakra as you continue to envision the gorgeous orange color of that chakra. Feel the orange energy pulsing beneath your hands in the chakra.

Next, repeat the seed mantra associated with the sacral chakra aloud, "Vam." As you say the word, feel your hands connect with the moving energy of the chakra beneath your skin. Repeat "Vam," and continue to be drawn into your awareness of your sacral chakra.

Repeat the mantra for as long as you'd like. You can do this mediation as frequently as you would like to strengthen this chakra. When you feel it is complete this time, bring your awareness back into the room. Focus on each sense and notice your surroundings. What do you see? Smell? Hear? Taste? Rub your arms and legs briskly and notice what you are feeling kinetically. Be certain you feel fully present to yourself before returning to your day. Drink plenty of water to help integrate the energies you gathered.

Your sacral chakra is associated with your ovaries or testicles. These endocrine glands are the ones that most govern this chakra. Endocrine glands produce hormones. The ovaries produce eggs to be fertilized and they also produce estrogen, progesterone, and testosterone. The testicles produce sperm and testosterone.

If these endocrine glands do not function correctly, impotence, low libido, and infertility can result. In modern life, we are exposed to myriad chemicals and xenoestrogens (fake estrogens). Xenoestrogens are substances that fool the body into thinking they are estrogen. Main sources of xenoestrogens are traditional household cleaning products like bleach, dry-cleaning chemicals, and plastics. Eliminating or reducing your exposure to these substances may help your body. Mind-body remedies for supporting these endocrine glands include guided visualization and acupuncture.

Other parts of the body associated with the sacral chakra are the uterus, genitals, kidneys, bladder, circulatory system, prostate, and sacral nerve plexus. Some potential signs of sacral chakra dysfunction include uterine, bladder, and prostate trouble; kidney illness; stiff lower back; and anemia.

Emotional, mental, and spiritual dysfunction of this chakra includes sex addiction, out of control emotions, or lack of emotion responsiveness.

To encourage health and vitality in this chakra, you can view clear, bright shades of orange, especially if you feel the chakra is underactive. You can also wear this color. You can wear a softer, more peachy orange to encourage the acceptance of life's sweetness. Since this chakra is specifically associated with life's simple pleasures, you can also engage in any activity that feels healthfully pleasurable for you.

EXERCISE: ACTIVITY TO CONNECT WITH YOUR SACRAL CHAKRA

Your sacral chakra is all about feeling good and experiencing sensory pleasure. It is also associated with the element of water. In this activity you will need sea salt, some uninterrupted time, and a bathtub or shower.

Draw yourself a bath if you have a tub. If you do not, do this same process standing in the shower. Get in and enjoy the feeling of the water on your skin. Really notice how warm it feels.

Now, grab your sea salt and use scoops of it on your arms and legs as an exfoliating scrub. Focus on the sensations on your skin. Notice if it feels good. Is it too rough? Or is it invigorating? Can you connect with your senses? Would you like to add a pleasant-smelling essential oil to this experience? Or drink some delicious tea and listen to some serene music? Focus on your five senses and listen to your body.

That is the essence of a healthy sacral chakra: being present to the sensory pleasure your body is experiencing. Tune in to these sensations and feel your sacral chakra strengthen.

SACRAL CHAKRA AFFIRMATION

"I FEEL PLEASURE TO MY CORE AND ALLOW MYSELF TO GAIN VITAL LIFE FORCE FROM IT."

5

MANIPURA— THE SOLAR PLEXUS CHAKRA

IN SANSKRIT THE WORD *MANIPURA* MEANS "LUS-trous gem." Manipura is a chakra located in your solar plexus—the area above your belly button and below your xiphoid process. Most traditions describe this chakra as yellow. Usually it is deemed to be a bright shade, full of vigor. One way that this chakra is judged to be healthy is if it is vibrantly colored and luminous. A great way to imagine the solar plexus chakra is as a brilliant yellow dynamo.

In Tantric traditions, the chakra is believed to be made of ten blue petals and a downward triangle with Hindu solar crosses, and a running ram at the base. In this book, we will focus on the Western model of thinking, which believes this chakra to be yellow.

Manipura governs your personal power, confidence, assertiveness, and will. This chakra is all about power. It empowers the rest of your body, and it relates to your right use of power and will. The solar plexus chakra creates your uniqueness and enables you to transform through your will and personal power. A bright and clear solar plexus chakra helps you wield your overall personal power in the world.

When in balance, this chakra emanates autonomy, self-esteem, confidence, and free will. It helps you be self-assured and independent in the world. It is meant to facilitate your meeting your own needs for validation and freedom. All people desire to feel sovereign and catalyzing to their own world. Because of these needs, it is a natural human urge to strengthen the solar plexus chakra.

Combustion is the solar plexus chakra's most influential force. It is the essence of transformation and power. It is the flame of metamorphosis. This chakra supplies your vim and vigor. It powers you up and fuels your action in the world. It's essential to accomplishing things that need a lot dynamic energy.

Your personal power is intrinsically important in your life. Ideally, your body will feel powerful and capable and your sense of self will be strong and healthy. This feeling stems from the energy of your solar plexus chakra. Power and balance in this chakra paves the way for a life of success and results.

EXERCISE: MEDITATION TO CONNECT WITH YOUR SOLAR PLEXUS CHAKRA

More awareness of your solar plexus chakra will help you feel confident and capable in the world. It will also bolster your connection to all of your chakras. It will open your eyes to the world of energy within you. Connection with your solar plexus chakra will help you be more conscious of your personal power.

Find a calm and quiet place where you will be able to enjoy solitude for about fifteen minutes. Relax into the space and breathe deeply. You may lie down or sit in meditation position with your legs crossed or sit in a chair, if you would like.

Close your eyes and relax into the rhythm of your breath moving in and out of your body. Let yourself relax into that feeling and beat. Allow the pace of your breathing to slow down a bit and become deeper.

In your inner vision now, see a glowing, vibrant yellow. It is made of light. Watch it glow before you. It might fill the screen of your mind or you may see it as a sphere or a mass of color energy. Let yourself go into this vibrant yellow. Feel its golden glow.

Next, place your hands on your solar plexus. Feel your hands connect to that chakra. Let your hands and Manipura exchange energy. And feel the pulse between the two. Notice the beautiful yellow color in that energy. Perceive its flavor.

Now, in your mind begin to repeat the seed mantra for this chakra, "Ram." Say the word aloud as you feel your hands connected the flowing, swirling energy of the chakra within you.

Keep repeating the mantra and feeling the power of this chakra for as long as you'd like. When you are ready to finish, remove your hands gently and bring your awareness back to the room you are in. Rub your arms and legs briskly and say aloud, "I am here now. I am present." Be sure you feel completely present to what is around you before going on with your day. Make sure to drink plenty of water today.

The solar plexus chakra is associated with your pancreas. This organ is an exocrine and endocrine gland. We will discuss its exocrine functions in a moment. As an endocrine gland, it secretes the hormones insulin and glucagon to control blood sugar levels.

Dysfunctions of this endocrine gland include hypoglycemia and type 1 diabetes. Hypoglycemia has many causes; one of the rarest is when the pancreas produces too much insulin. With type 1 diabetes, it does not produce enough. Mind-body remedies to help with both of these include tai chi, yoga, and Ayurveda (a Hindu system of medicine that is based on the idea of balance in all bodily systems and proper diet, herbal treatments, and yogic breathing).

Other parts of the body associated with this chakra are the overall digestive system and muscles as well as the exocrine functions of the pancreas, which excretes enzymes to break down proteins, lipids, carbohydrates, and nucleic acids in food. Some body-based chakra dysfunction includes ulcers and digestive disorders.

Emotional, spiritual, and mental dysfunction of this chakra is often in the form or excess anger and rage, whether repressed or inappropriately expressed. Typically, people with a "short fuse" need to balance and soothe their solar plexus chakra. Anger management skills can be learned from a qualified professional.

Health and wellness of this chakra can be increased by visually taking in shades of clear yellow. If the chakra is overactive and too much rage and anger are present, then clear pastel yellow can soothe the energy center and help it relax. If the chakra is under-active and you need more confidence to magnify your charm or personal power, then shades of bright, clear, strong, vibrant yellow will be helpful.

To increase the health of the solar plexus chakra, vigorous exercise can be helpful. So can strength training of all kinds. Building your stamina, endurance, and strength all help this chakra function with clarity and ease. Another major way to bol-ster this chakra is to put extra emphasis on building your self-esteem. Quick ways to do this are: become aware of your inner critic and try to replace those thoughts with positive ones, and create a list of at least thirty wonderful things about yourself. Treat yourself with kindness and respect, and your solar plexus chakra will have an opportunity to clear and strengthen.

Since your will is centered in your solar plexus chakra, it is a very important energy center to have in healthy balance because it affects your ability to push your creations out into the world and move them forward. Your third chakra is a big part of your suc-cess in the world. In our society, will energy moves situations in the direction you desire. This has an effect on your career among other things in your life.

You can use your will to move things forward as long as you balance that will by always insuring and intending that every-thing that transpires is for the highest good of all life, including you. Look for win/win situations in response to circumstances in your life and then know that your will can be strong and indi-viduated, and allow it to flow in the direction you want. It is just like a river of vibration and you can create and step into the infi-nite, dazzling flow and harness the power of your will to create your best life.

EXERCISE: ACTIVITY TO CONNECT WITH YOUR SOLAR PLEXUS CHAKRA

One of the primary reasons the solar plexus chakra becomes blocked or too dense is the repression of rage or anger. Repressing anger is a completely natural thing to do and almost everyone does it to some degree. The renowned orthopedist Dr. John Sarno has devoted his entire career to the study of the role of repressed emotion in healing the body.

As a medical intuitive for over fifteen years, Amy, one of the authors of this book, has noticed that the most common place where people stuff their repressed anger is in the deep interior of the solar plexus chakra. In this activity, you will easily give a release valve to that denser energy and as a result free up that space for lighter energy of strength and confidence.

Find a secluded area where you can be unobserved and preferably a little bit loud. If you can, find a spot outside that is ideal, but indoors (ideally on a ground floor) will also work. During the exercise you are going to be expelling your anger and rage into the Earth. The Earth can recycle any energy that is generated by humans, plants, or animals. So, in this case the Earth will absorb your anger and recycle it into white light that it will then use as fuel. It is a mutually beneficial arrangement between you and the Earth.

Stand tall and close your eyes. Breathe deeply into your abdomen and begin to stomp your feet. Now, stop stomping and, on your next big inhale, envision the breath coming into you. When you exhale sharply, see it coming out of your solar plexus and beginning to form a storm cloud in front of your body. Repeat this process and keep inhaling and exhaling and growing your storm cloud in front of you.

When it is fully formed, on your next big inhale, really feel it in your solar plexus. Then, with a forceful exhalation, envision a bolt of lightning coming out of the storm cloud and going straight down into the Earth. Do this repeatedly and keep snapping lightning down into the Earth. This is your repressed anger. Just let it go. Keep going and exhale sharply and send the lightning down. You can also clap your hands, shout, and stomp your feet. Allow yourself to truly let go and release all the pent-up feelings within you. You will not know what they are all about. That is okay and it's actually more efficient that way. Keep your mind out of it and be in your body. Keep doing this for as long as you'd like, and when it is complete, you will know because you will feel the process wind down. You may get tired before you finish and need to do this exercise multiple times. That is okay, too. There is no rush.

When you are ready to wind it down, let your breathing return to normal and take a few moments to sit down and wrap your arms around yourself and give yourself a hug. Then make any notes about how you are feeling in your journal. If this process brings a lot up for you, consider talking to a trusted friend or a qualified professional as needed.

Be sure to drink lots of water after and treat yourself with kindness and care.

SOLAR PLEXUS CHAKRA AFFIRMATION

"I AM CONFIDENT AND I STAND IN MY POWER."

6

ANAHATA— THE HEART CHAKRA

THE SANSKRIT TRANSLATION OF THE WORD *anahata* is "unstruck"—meaning a sound that is made without any two things striking. The heart chakra is located in the center of the chest. Western traditions describe it as green in color. It is generally thought to be bright emerald green. The brighter and more full of light the color is, the healthier the chakra.

In Tantric traditions, it is believed to have twelve deep red petals surrounding a six-pointed star. For the rest of this chapter, we will be focusing on the Western ideas pertaining to this chakra.

Anahata rules love, breath, balance, relationships, and unity. This chakra is all about the higher energies of love and compassion when in balance. It governs matters of romance and friendship and heart connection. When your heart chakra's need are met, you feel loved, cared for, and you love yourself. The universal urge that we all have to love and be loved originates in the heart chakra.

This chakra's most influential force is equilibrium, which means a state of balance and calmness. This is type of emotional stability and symmetry. Having a calm and content heart is the essence of the balanced heart chakra's equilibrium.

Love and a happy heart are crucial to your quality of life. Life is about connection and caring, and without it, you feel bereft and alone. A healthy heart chakra lets you know that you are never alone. You can extend caring to others and yourself and allow your heart to be open and full.

EXERCISE: MEDITATION TO CONNECT WITH YOUR HEART CHAKRA

Connecting with your heart chakra will help you give and receive love more freely, develop greater levels of compassion of yourself and others, and feel more open and connected to the world around you. When you tune in to your heart chakra, you realize the world is a largely benevolent place and that we are all interconnected.

Find a quiet spot and sit or lie down. Make sure you will remain undisturbed for about fifteen minutes. Start by closing your eyes and relaxing your body. Rest and relax into the floor or chair beneath you and start breathing more deeply.

After you have relaxed your body and done a few minutes of deep breathing, allow yourself to picture a gorgeous wash of the brightest emerald green before you. Watch this color pulse with life. Pink is also associated with this chakra, so allow any soft, rosy colors to swirl in too. Stay focused on the colors before you and allow yourself to feel them pulsing with life.

Now, bring your hands up to the center of your chest and place them palm-to-palm with your fingers pointing upward. Feel the green and rose of your heart pulsing in the center of your chest and notice how your hands are engulfed in that pulsing. Immerse yourself in the colors and let them fill your senses. Your hands may be tingling, warm, or pulsing with energy because they are so connected to your heart. The energy of your heart often flows down your arms and out your hands. Some examples are when you pat someone you love on the shoulder, you stroke a child's hair, or you give your spouse a neck massage.

Stay focused on the colors and sensations and now begin to repeat the seed mantra, internally or aloud. It is "Yam." Repeat it and focus on your hands connecting to your heart. Feel the colors there. Sense the emotions in your heart. Let your awareness rest in that area, breathe deeply, and feel the pulsing there.

Continue repeating the mantra and feeling your heart for as long as you'd like. When the process feels complete, let your awareness come back to the room and your surroundings. Pat your arms and legs vigorously and say to yourself, "I am here now. I am present." Drink some extra water and continue your day with a feeling of love in your heart.

The heart chakra is associated with your thymus gland. Your thymus is most active before puberty. It's seated between your lungs, behind your sternum. Before puberty, your thymus produces lots of thymosin, a hormone that helps your body produce T-cells, which play a vital role in immunity for your whole lifetime.

Endocrine dysfunction associated with the thymus gland can involve lowered immunity. Since most of the thymus's influence happens in childhood, the best way to strengthen the body as an adult is to boost immunity in myriad ways. Two mind-body remedies that can help are meditation and qigong to reduce the effects of stress on your body. General exercise also helps boost immunity and dry skin brushing may also help.

The other parts of the body associated with the heart chakra are the heart, lungs, hands, and arms. Some potential signs of heart chakra imbalance are heart disease and asthma. Emotional dysfunction of the chakra can include fear of not being loved enough and not being able to fully receive love from others.

To promote health in your heart chakra, you simply must immerse yourself in love in a balanced and healthy way. A great way to give and receive unconditional love is with pet dogs. If you have a dog, you likely already know what this feels like. If you don't, you might want to spend time with a friend's dog and offer the pet your love and caring. Spending time with kids in your family, especially those who are in early or middle childhood, is another great way to share feelings of love in an easy, organic manner. Deep breathing exercises can be helpful and many people report great results using the Emotional Freedom Technique, also known as EFT.

EXERCISE: ACTIVITY TO CONNECT WITH YOUR HEART CHAKRA

The heart chakra's natural state is open and relaxed. In our fast-paced world, filled with sarcasm and snarky comments, it can be challenging to keep it that way. But ultimately, an open heart feels better. Closing your heart just interferes with your enjoyment of life and potentially your health. So, take the time to ponder what opens your heart. It will be things that inspire feelings of love and caring inside of you. Make a list now of what does that for you and commit to prioritizing opening your heart. Every day, try to open a little bit more. If you are afraid of getting hurt, acknowledge that, but ask yourself if it is worth living your life in a manner where you miss out on love and caring available for you to give and receive. Love is worth the risk.

Remember that loving yourself is just as important as loving others. Your heart chakra functions most healthfully when you give yourself regular love and caring. That can mean treating yourself to a relaxing massage but also setting appropriate boundaries with loved ones to safeguard your time and energy.

Now we will do an activity to activate the infinite nature

of your heart chakra. Find a quiet spot where you will be undisturbed and lie down. Allow about twenty minutes to experience this process.

Quiet your mind by breathing deeply and focusing on the feeling of the air moving in and out of your mouth. Let yourself fall into that rhythm and relax deeply. Think back to the list you made earlier of things that inspire the feeling of love in your heart. Pick one of those and imagine it to conjure up the emotion and energy of love now. Really hone in on it and make the love feeling radiate through you. It feels like a feeling and an energy simultaneously.

Now, let it pulse from the center of your chest and repeat the word "Love" over and over in your mind as you feel the emotion and energy. Pulse the energy out around you to encompass your entire body. Breathe and repeat the word "Love."

Now, expand it out in the same way so it is a bubble about three feet around you on all sides. Breathe and feel this love that you are giving to yourself.

Next, picture your town or city on a map. Take in a huge inhale and repeat the word "love" in your mind as you exhale for as long as you are able and envision your love bubble expanding instantly and quickly to encompass your entire town. Once it has expanded, feel it pulsing love from your heart to your entire town.

Now, picture the Earth! Feel the love pulsing in your heart. Notice how it pulses through your body, the area around your body, and your town. Inhale deeply, and as you exhale, allow your love bubble to swiftly inflate and instantaneously grow to envelope the entire planet. Feel the love in your heart engulfing the whole Earth. Notice what this feels like? Does it evoke even more emotion in your heart and body?

This love for the entire planet is the essence of compassion, which is the heart chakra's highest expression. Bathe in the feeling.

When you are ready, you can bring your awareness back into the room. Wiggle your fingers and toes and look around you. Rub your limbs briskly and clap your hands to make sure you are feeling fully present. Be sure to drink some extra water today.

HEART CHAKRA AFFIRMATION

"I OPEN MY HEART TO THE IMMENSE LOVE IN MY LIFE."

VISHUDDHA— THE THROAT CHAKRA

T HE FIFTH CHAKRA IS CALLED *VISHUDDHA*, which means "purification." It's located in the throat and is blue in the Western chakra system. The Hindus originally described it as a whitish circular shape made up of sixteen purple and smoky gray petals. The gray comes from its association with the elephant Airavata, lord of all herbivorous animals. Within this circular shape is a blue triangle with a white circle. The circle references a full moon, and the moon can symbolize the invisible ether or etheric energy, itself connected to dreaming. Therefore, the throat chakra is also associated with dream yoga, or dreaming in general.

The major association of the throat chakra is with speech, communication, and creative expression. When the throat chakra is clear and open, we are able to let things go, especially our own past choices for good or ill, and express our views in a healthy way. We learn our lessons and move on; there's no dwelling on the past, present, or future anxieties, and we've gained wisdom from life experience. Our speech flows freely, we live in a state of healthy detachment, and this detachment makes it easier to experience powerful spirit dreams. The "ether" associated with the throat chakra is akin to our astral body, and at night it's believed that this etheric body leaves the body to dream.

On the other hand, when the throat chakra is blocked, the opposite is true. Our personal expression is limited, and we are wracked with guilt and shame over the past, fear the future, and find it difficult to live in the present moment. The roots of the word Vishuddha are "visha" and "shuddhi." Visha means "poison" and shuddhi means "purification." Therefore, when this chakra is closed, it is believed to become a poison in the body resulting in ageing and death. When it's open and clear, it's seen as a purification agent that may contribute to exceptional longevity.

Resonance is this chakra's biggest influence. When our throat energy flows freely, we feel confident in who we are and easily share our voice with the world around us.

This chakra has a seed mantra sound associated with it, "Ham." It's pronounced "hahmm" rather than ham, like the pig. If you feel your throat chakra is blocked, repeating this mantra during meditation is believed to help purify it. Other means of clearing out the throat include headstands, such as yoga asanas like salamba sirsasana, the "king of asanas." Singing in general is also believed to be a healthy activity for the throat, whether in a dedicated kirtan active meditation or just singing along to your favorite song on the radio.

Before we jump into our first throat chakra meditation, let's look a bit deeper at a more esoteric side of the throat chakra called Dream Yoga. Dream Yoga is a very important part of Tibetan Buddhist practice, and it is seen as an important stepping stone on the path of transcendence from the endless cycles of birth and death. Many Eastern religions believe that we exist in an elaborate dream that only appears to be "real."

Working with dreams is believed to be an excellent way of realizing that our waking lives, too, are only dreams. This is accomplished by developing lucid dreaming, or waking up in a dream while the body remains asleep. Once lucid dreaming can be induced at will, it is possible to direct the course of dreams for spiritual benefit. The practices take years to master and are very elaborate, but Tibetan monks believe that mastering dreams prepares humans for the intense tidal wave of visual and sensory manifestations which occur just after death. Buddhist monks believe that we become entranced with these post-mortem manifestations and are drawn back into a new incarnation. However, if we can transcend these illusory, dreamlike images then we have a chance of breaking the endless cycle of death and rebirth.

In the throat chakra lie the beginnings of dream yoga practice. There are many visualizations, mantras, yogic, breathing, and other practices that rely on an active and healthy throat chakra for their successful completion. It's a fascinating aspect of Buddhism that is only now becoming more popular in the west.

EXERCISE: THROAT MEDITATION

Let's do a meditation to help us connect with the feelings and energies of the throat chakra. Find a quiet, comfortable place to either sit or lie down where you won't be disturbed or distracted. Take several breaths to calm down and focus your attention in this present moment, right where you are. Be aware of your body, your clothes, your breath, and the way your body feels. Continue breathing slowly with a gentle inhalation and a gentle exhalation. Be aware of the room or space you're in, how it feels, sounds, and smells. If you're not already doing so, be sure to breathe with a smile on your face. It doesn't have to be a huge grin; a subtle smile is easiest to maintain but helps put the mind in the proper mental space for the meditation.

Imagine your body surrounded by a ball of light. You pull the light in toward your body with each inhale and expand it out again with every exhale. Spend several breaths expanding and contracting the ball of light around you. This helps you learn to feel your auric field, the natural field of life energy that surrounds and penetrates your body. Your chakras are a part of this field. Continue smiling.

On your next breath, focus your attention on the energy around your throat. Simply paying attention to your throat may make it feel like it's humming or buzzing with energy. Again, on the inhale pull the energy around your throat in to the center of your throat and on the exhale expand it again. Continue doing this breathing meditation until you feel a bright happy feeling in your throat, as if you could squeal with joy, or until it feels tired from the exercise. If your throat feels tired after a while, not to worry. Take a break and continue practicing another day, until eventually you feel that excited, happy feeling in your throat. Continue smiling.

When you do feel exuberant in your throat, which may sound like an odd feeling until you've actually experienced it, you've increased and purified the energy in your throat. Congratulations! There's one more step to ensure the throat energy remains balanced with the rest of your auric field. Inhale slowly once again and place your attention on your throat, then exhale and imagine the energy in your throat moving down the center of your body toward your belly. Let it sit in your belly through the exhalation. Continue this practice until the energy in your throat feels calm once again. Continue smiling, and when you feel ready, stretch your arms and legs and move your body around for a few minutes to bring your awareness back to your entire body.

The thyroid is the endocrine gland associated with the throat chakra. It's located in the throat, just below and to either side of the voice box. Thyroid hormones have many body regulation functions, mainly metabolism and body temperature during adulthood, but also have a great role in the healthy growth of the body during childhood development. Thyroid imbalance has unfortunately become all too common in the twenty-first century, especially for women.

Because of its location, the throat chakra has always been linked with hearing and the ears, and speech and the mouth. For the symbolic reasons mentioned above, the throat chakra is also counterintuitively linked to dreaming and the etheric body. Another interesting throat chakra association is with overall quality of life. Vishuddha has poisonous and purifying aspects; it's indicated in the name itself. From the earliest Indian writings about vishuddha, it was believed that the state of health or dysfunction of the throat chakra was directly linked to the quality of one's life. A closed throat chakra can lead to the ruin of one's livelihood, whereas a healthy chakra supports qualities of leadership and success.

In the Western system, the throat chakra is mainly associated with clear communication and emotional expression. When the throat chakra is out of balance, there is stilted speech and emotional expression is dampened. Fear can be a major factor in both conditions and therefore facing fears is seen as a good way to open up the throat chakra.

EXERCISE: ACTIVITY TO CONNECT WITH THE THROAT CHAKRA

Let's do an easy exercise to help us connect with the throat chakra. In this exercise we'll use the voice to open and clear the energy in the throat. Find a comfortable place to sit where you won't be distracted, and take several deep slow breaths to relax. Place your awareness firmly in the moment. Be aware of your body, your arms, legs, head, and neck. Follow the rise and fall of your breathing. Feel the clothes on your skin, the chair, pillows, or floor on which you're sitting. Notice the sounds, smells, temperature, and other sensory information around you. Continue breathing and be present.

The sound of the throat chakra is "Ham," pronounced "hahmm," sort of like the word "hum." Inhale deeply, calmly, slowly, hold the breath for a moment, and then upon a slow exhalation, say "Ham," letting the sound linger over the entire exhalation. Let the sound of Ham reverberate through your throat. It is believed this sounds helps activate the energy of the throat chakra, cleansing it of stagnant energy and helping it flow clear and strong.

If you're new to reciting this mantra, after a short time your throat may actually begin to feel sore. This may be from a combination of sore throat muscles and the moving of old stagnant energy in the throat. There's no need to push through the discomfort; simply stop and pick it up again next time. The more your practice, the stronger your throat energy will feel.

Actually, any type of singing will activate the energy of the throat chakra. Singing positive words, affirmations, or songs is best. It doesn't matter what language you use; it's the feeling behind the words that counts. Singing songs of hope, love, inspiration, joy, and happiness has a generally positive effect on your entire energy field and is especially beneficial to the throat chakra.

THROAT CHAKRA AFFIRMATION

"I EXPRESS MYSELF WITH EASE AND GRACE."

AJNA—
THE THIRD EYE
CHAKRA

THE NEXT CHAKRA IS CALLED *AJNA*, WHICH means "command." It is located between the brows, above the eyes, and near the top of the spine and has an indigo blue color in the modern Western system. In the traditional view, the Ajna chakra is white in color with two petals on either side. These petals symbolize a pair of nadis running up either side of the body that connect near the Ajna chakra. They are said to end at the nostrils.

The word *Ajna* means both self-command, achieved by overcoming the illusion of duality, and also the deep surrendering to the command or guidance of the guru. Ultimately, your own liberated self is the true guru, but until then, a guru is your selfless spiritual teacher.

When the Ajna chakra is activated, it is believed to coincide with a point in the spiritual development of a person where duality is overcome. So the Ajna chakra governs spiritual awakening. Its keyword is illumination. Attachment to the transient world around us fades and a unified mental state emerges. In the traditional Hindu view, when the third eye is awakened, it is possible to quickly burn through past karma, detach from the illusory sufferings of the world, and find true inner peace. Where an activated throat chakra indicates the achievement of a high level of self-purification, the third eye chakra's activation yields transcendence.

Psychic abilities, or siddhis, come alive with a fully activated third eye chakra. These are not mental powers, as the chakras do not correlate to the physical body. Rather, think of the chakras as pieces of a spiritual dynamo, that, when connected, bring about an energetic transformation of consciousness. In the process of spiritual awakening, the body is also transformed as a whole. Many people desire psychic ability and it is a completely natural phenomenon. As discussed in *The Way of the Psychic Heart* by Chad Mercree, everyone is born with these abilities; it is only a matter of practice to activate them. When the Ajna chakra is spontaneously awakened, however, the psychic abilities can come all at once. The experience can be overwhelming, and in the traditional view in order to move past the third eye chakra and into the crown chakra, it is necessary to overcome all attachments to the siddhis. Psychic abilities can have a powerful effect on our life experience and letting go of what may feel like omniscient powers can be a difficult task.

Light is the third eye chakra's driving force, as both sunlight and the light of consciousness and illumination.

EXERCISE: THIRD EYE MEDITATION

Let's get to know our third eye chakra center by doing the following meditation. As usual, find a comfortable place to meditate. For this meditation it doesn't matter if you sit in a chair or on the floor, stand, or lie down. Take several deep breaths to relax and feel centered. Now, take several deep breaths through the heart. On the inhale, imagine your breath pulling in to your heart and filling it up. Now, slowly exhale and let the heart-breath expand out through your body. Repeat this several times until you feel a deeper level of peace and relaxation.

Now that you're relaxed and centered, bring your awareness up to your eyes. On the next inhale, imagine the breath filling the space between your eyes. Feel the energy in the breath filling the space with light. Hold the breath for a moment before exhaling. On the exhale, feel the energy in your third eye expand outward. Repeat several times.

The seed mantra sound for the third eye chakra is "Aum," or "Om." On the next exhale chant the word Aum, letting every sound express itself fully—Ahhhh-ooooooh-mmmmmmmm. Repeat the seed mantra for the next several long, slow exhalations. Can you feel the energy of the third eye chakra moving?

Breathing into the chakras is an easy way to help people learn to feel energy moving within each chakra. There is energy in the breath and it can be moved, similar to chi, anywhere the attention brings it. In this case, we're moving the energy to the third eye chakra. At first, after several breaths, the third eye area may become sensitive. Simply stop whenever you wish and practice again another day.

The third eye chakra is associated with the pineal and pituitary glands in contemporary Western systems. The pituitary is a "master" gland that regulates many hormonal functions in the body by sending signals to other glands in the body to produce hormones. Without the pituitary, the thyroid, adrenals, ovaries, and testes. It's also responsible for releasing human growth hormone throughout our lives, regulating everything from overall growth to muscle and bone mass. The pituitary also regulates water balance and the production of milk in breastfeeding women.

The pineal gland controls sleep patterns and some sex hormones. In some more primitive species of animals, the pineal gland is a type of vestigial eye.

These glandular associations were not present in the earliest Tantric teachings but have developed over time. They are especially popular in contemporary Western systems. That's one of the most exciting things about working with chakras. Our understanding of what they are and how they function has progressed through the centuries as people from all over the world continue to investigate chakras. Whereas the Tantric system symbolically linked chakras with many different colors and shapes, various Sanskrit symbols, deities and sounds, in the Western system the associations are more connected to parts of the body, rainbow colors, elements, sounds, astrological symbols, and even Kabballah mythology.

EXERCISE: ACTIVITY TO CONNECT WITH YOUR THIRD-EYE CHAKRA

This exercise will help you connect with your third-eye chakra. We'll start as before with finding a comfortable place to practice, and by taking several deep breaths to relax and get centered. Become aware of your body, your arms and legs, and your head and shoulders. Breathe into each part of your body and let it relax more deeply with each exhalation.

Bring your attention to your third eye chakra. Breathe in and out of your third eye a few times until you feel its energy moving. When this happens, you will feel a buzzing or tingling between your brows, your thoughts may quiet, and you will feel exceptionally present. Let this buzzing, tingling sensation build until it's almost unbearable.

Now, form an intention about something you wish to come to pass. State it to yourself or aloud. You create your reality from every thought, word, and deed. The third eye chakra represents that part of ourselves that manifests intention by being able to tune in to our inner divine wisdom, our intuition. When we activate our third eye chakra, this helps develop a strong active connection to our intuitive abilities. Ask yourself what the next steps are to achieving your intention. Allow yourself to see the next three steps to take toward your goal. Write these steps down and make it a point to take action on these steps, one by one. When they're completed, repeat this activity until your goals are achieved.

You can do a similar practice with memories. Repeat the first two paragraphs of this activity and then try to recall something lost to your everyday memory. Ask yourself about a specific period of time or event and then allow the energy of the third eye chakra to help you recall specifics about these events.

In traditional Tantric practice, the chakras are activated one at a time from the root to the crown. As each chakra activates, spontaneous personality, physical, emotional, mental, and spiritual changes occur on the path toward enlightenment. For the third eye chakra, these onset of psychic abilities is a true hallmark of its activation. It's been described as the union of opposites, where pleasure and detachment live in perfect harmony. This union paves the way for the expression of the crown chakra, the ultimate expression of kundalini life-energy and consciousness.

THIRD EYE CHAKRA AFFIRMATION

"MY INTUITION GUIDES ME FOR MY HIGHEST GOOD."

9

SAHASRARA— THE CROWN CHAKRA

THE CROWN CHAKRA IS THE LAST AND SEVenth energy center in most traditional chakra systems. Its Sanskrit name is *Sahasrara*, meaning "thousand-petalled," in reference to the infinite petals visualized with this chakra in the traditional system. Tibetan Buddhists imagine it with thirty-two petals, and it varies from tradition to tradition. In the Western system, it is seen as violet or white. The crown is located at the top of the head, in the place where our soft spot used to be when we were babies. Where the petals of the other chakras are typically drawn pointing up, the crown points down.

At its highest expression the crown chakra represents enlightenment, pure awareness, and an ability to escape from the endless cycles of birth and death from which most of us suffer. However, for us regular mortals it is also connected with inspiration and creativity, similar to the third eye chakra.

The consciousness of the crown chakra is beyond all duality, all grasping for temporal things like love, success, and so on. A person with an activated crown chakra can be described as glowing, literally. Life is lived fully aware in each moment, desiring nothing and appreciating every new moment and the experiences they bring. It's a state of consciousness wholly foreign to most of us, but to many Eastern traditions it represents the goal of the human experience and is believed to be possible to achieve in a single lifetime.

An out of balance crown chakra leads to insanity, the god complex of an unfortunately high number of contemporary gurus. Drugs are a huge hindrance to the development of chakras and the healthy expression of kundalini life-force energy, and part of this is because of the way drugs alter the human energy field. They can blow open the third eye chakra and allow the unprepared to experience psychic phenomenon in an unhealthy way, and they can also alter the expression of the crown chakra and make people feel like gods or goddesses when in reality they are anything but.

When properly activated, illumination is the key influential force of the crown chakra. Its essence connects us to the divine, to the entire cosmos. Or rather, its awakening allows us to remember the connections we've had all along to everything in existence.

There is no seed mantra, or sound, associated with the crown chakra. It is beyond all expression, and in a way represents the void between all things, the pause between the inhale and the exhale of creation. The moment between all things—that's how the crown chakra is connected to the All, through the in-between spaces between every manifested thing.

EXERCISE: MEDITATION TO CONNECT WITH THE CROWN CHAKRA

Find a comfortable place to sit or lie down and relax. Take several deep, slow breaths and with each exhalation let your body become more and more relaxed. Feel your body, your hands and feet, arms and legs, and neck and head. Continue breathing. Starting with the root chakra, take a deep breath into each chakra, hold for a few moments, and then exhale. As you move up your body feel all the chakras connected, different parts of your single energy field. Follow the chakras up one by one toward your crown. Feel their energy come alive with the breath. Feel your energy increase and flow more freely with each new connection. Feel the energy of your heart enfold you with love. Move to your throat and third eye chakras and feel peacefulness side by side with the love. Now, take several more breaths and connect with your crown.

Feel the expanded awareness of your crown energy merge with that sense of loving peacefulness. It's a beautiful experience, a subtle taste of your future enlightened self. If at any time you develop a headache or feel undue pressure in your head, simply breathe all the energy you've just built up back down to your root chakra and when the discomfort subsides stop the practice. Over time, you'll be able to hold the energy in your crown for longer periods of time.

If there is no discomfort, let yourself bask in the wonderful and blissful feelings of an opening crown chakra. It is unique, a combination of peacefulness, lovingkindness, and pleasure all rolled into one. When you are finished, let all the energy in your crown fall back down where it needs to go with each exhalation. If your energy is flowing well, there is no need to tell it where to go; it will go where it's needed on its own.

For each of the previous chakras there has been a corresponding part of the endocrine system to which most contemporary practitioners agree. However, this is not the case with the crown chakra. It has been linked to the entire endocrine system as well as specifically to the pineal and pituitary glands and to the hypothalamus region of the brain. The traditional yogic lore of Swami Ranganathananda (1908–2005) has a different idea about the crown chakra. He writes, "Yogis speak of a subtle nerve going to the crown of the head known as Susumna, which is located in the center of the spinal column. When the life energy of a Yogi, it is believed, passes through the susumna and goes through the aperture in the crown of the head, known as *brahma-randhra* or 'the opening leading to Braham'—he will not be reborn in the world, but will steadily reach brahmaloka, the world of the cosmic Mind . . . The path thus traversed is known as the 'the northern path' or 'the path of light.'" This "subtle nerve" is part of the human energy field and is not connected to any particular gland in the body.

Students who work with the crown chakra need to be mindful of its instability in the beginning of a spiritual practice. It is possible to open the crown chakra too far but not yet know how to close it back down. This can lead to sensitivity to light and sound, headaches, and other physical symptoms. It is best to work with the crown chakra under the guidance of an experienced teacher to avoid these unpleasant experiences. Therefore, the following activity will help you connect to the spirit of the crown chakra indirectly, through active participation in service to humanity.

EXERCISE: ACTIVITY TO CONNECT TO THE CROWN CHAKRA

Part of what the crown chakra represents is that becoming enlightened means transcending worldly concerns, especially of the self. Ideally, there would never be an enlightened spiritual guru who would care about fame and fortune, the accumulation of material things, or holding power over throngs of adoring followers. Such things simply have lost interest for an enlightened person. However, enlightened people exhibit traits of deep concern and compassion for the suffering of fellow beings, human and otherwise. The achievement of universal consciousness as symbolized by the crown chakra is always linked to a compassionate and caring being. Different systems around the world visualize the shape of the crown chakra differently, from a bell to a multipetalled crown to a conical wheel of white light. As with all the chakras, there isn't always consensus about the details or symbology of each chakra but there does seem to be consensus about their functions and qualities.

A wonderful way to express the qualities of an activated crown chakra is by attending to the suffering of humanity. Becoming a fully spiritually awakened being has its dangers, including the temptation of hanging onto ego's great need for self-aggrandizement. You can't bring your normal little self with you on the path for enlightenment. We are all idiots in one way or another, all because of an unhealthy attachment to our ego. The ego cares so much about how we look, what we earn, who we know, how far up the social chain we are, and other silly nonsense. To bring this attitude with you on a spiritual quest spells certain ruin. Therefore, focus instead on service to other. Your needs can wait; tend to those closest to you first, and then to others. Similar to the heart chakra, cultivate kindness and love toward all and your enlightenment will last forever. Paradoxically, an activated crown chakra comes with a deep sense of sorrow for the suffering of humanity, and being of service helps take the sting from the sorrow.

CROWN CHAKRA AFFIRMATION

"I EASILY CONNECT WITH UNIVERSAL LIFE FORCE."

10

ADDITIONAL CHAKRAS

MANY PEOPLE INTERESTED IN CHAKRAS OR energy healing have heard there are seven chakras going from the base of the spine to the top of the head. You might be surprised to learn that many traditions described many other chakras throughout the body. Some are said to be located between the traditional seven while others are placed all over the body. Let's investigate some of the more well-known "other" chakras we can use to feel more grounded, enhance our healing practice, and bring about a greater understanding of our spiritual potential.

A popular additional chakra is called the Earth star chakra. This name has been mentioned in several contemporary sources and is described as being six inches to four feet below the body. Since the human energy field extends in all directions around us, it also extends underground when we walk the Earth. People use the Earth star chakra to connect deeply into the center of the planet, to help increase feelings of being grounded and present and to engage in contemporary shamanic work.

As below, so above. Beyond the crown chakra, many traditions see additional chakras extending above the crown chakra, and the number varies by tradition, usually five or seven, though in some traditions it runs as high as thirteen. Many modern New Age groups have attributed angelic or archangelic qualities to these additional chakras but in Hindu, Tibetan, and Taoist systems they're seen as simple extensions of the human energy field. With advanced yogic practice, students who gather enough energy in the body, or who have opened up and cleared their lower chakras, are able to experience the qualities of these additional chakras.

While healthy, fully activated chakras are associated with the onset of various psychic abilities, when the next realm of chakras above the physical body are activated, an even more rarified state of spiritual existence is believed to be activated. The opening of these higher chakras is very pleasant and comforting, and even though advanced psychic abilities can be achieved and sometimes spontaneously occur, spiritual detachment is at an all-time high so there is no desire to pursue these experiences. The irony is that many spiritual seekers start out hoping to achieve spiritual bliss, enlightenment with all its fabled powers, yet the closer we come to enlightenment the less we care about such things.

When these higher chakras are awakened there is also an unmistakable experience of complete groundedness, as if we've come fully into ourselves for the first time. Issues that once concerned us no longer hold any allure, and all seems right with the world no matter how much darkness exists before us. It is easier to express all the positive qualities of the lower chakras. There is a sweetness to life that didn't exist before and being of service, living from compassion, is as natural as taking a breath. It is really one of the loveliest experiences to surrender deep enough to the present moment that the higher chakras bloom like a hierarchy of flowers. This joyful feeling is also part of the illusion of being alive, but how sweet it is while it lasts.

Eventually even these expressions of awareness fade as spiritual awakening expands to a calmer, more subdued next step. I don't know of any practices to develop the higher chakras; as the lower ones open and are cleansed, the higher ones begin to manifest and bubble open, one after the next.

In between these higher and lower sets of chakras are countless additional chakras sprinkled in between the original seven. The number, location, importance, and qualities of these additional chakras vary widely even within the same tradition. For example, in Hindu philosophy, different gurus throughout the centuries have written contradictory texts about additional chakras in the body. The numbers range from a few to hundreds of additional points. Perhaps some of these points relate to acupuncture points in traditional Chinese medicine. The origins of chakras are very intellectual and this can lead to getting lost in layers of detail that don't apply to the average person. Something the contemporary New Age movement has contributed to the understanding of chakras is the way they embrace a simple and direct experience of chakras as bundles of energy. This has led to a more heartfelt and emotional approach to energy healing.

Minor chakras that are pivotal in your experience of life exist in the hands and feet. Your hand chakras are an extension of the heart chakra. They are one of the parts of the body that most interacts with your world. They pat someone's arm to show caring or punctuate a point. They prepare your food and order your life. They high-five a friend to punctuate an exciting moment. Through the hand chakras you share and accept energy from your world. You may feel your hand chakras as pulsing, warm, or tingling when activated. They are a way you get to share your love with the world in a nonverbal manner.

Your feet chakras provide a touchstone between you and the earth. They are connected with your root chakra and Earth star chakra and act as your interface between the physical body and the Earth below that supports it. A wonderful way to active your foot chakras is reflexology. If you work at a desk all day and want to feel more grounded, you can place a discreet foot massager under your desk and stimulate the chakras in your feet while you work to create a greater sense of balance and harmony.

ADDITIONAL CHAKRA AFFIRMATION

"ALL OF MY CHAKRAS ARE INFUSED WITH LIGHT AND HEALTH."

QUIZ

TO OPTIMIZE YOUR CHAKRAS
AND YOUR LIFE

So much of your day is influenced by the healthy flow of your chakras. The more open and dynamic your chakras are, the more the good things in life can flow to you. In this chapter, you will learn how one or more chakras can affect various parts of your life and how to optimize your energy centers. Take the quiz and see how many questions you answer "yes" to and then go to the corresponding exercise following to learn how to rebalance that area of your life. You can refer back to this quiz again and again at different times to tune up any chakras that are ready for optimization.

1. Do you feel over-simulated and tense around crowds, loud noises, and bright lights?

If you answered yes, then you may need to seal your space. Turn to Exercise One in this chapter to learn how.

2. Do you over identify with other people's feelings to the point where you are frequently worrying about other's emotional states at the expense of your own?

If you answered yes, then you may need to disconnect nightly. Turn to Exercise Two to learn how.

3. Do you feel fuzzy and sore in your forehead as well as irritable and spacey?

If you answered yes, then you may need to smudge your third eye. Turn to Exercise Three to learn how.

4. When you speak in a group do people often not hear you or tell you to speak up?

If yes, then you may need to project your true voice. Turn to Exercise Four to learn how.

5. Do you feel like you are going through the motions of life but you are actually somewhere else?

If you answered yes, then you may need to reengage your root vitality. Turn to Exercise Five to learn how.

6. Do you suffer from nightmares or generally experience restless sleep?

If you answered yes, you may need to learn how to seal your auric field at night through intention and the creation of sacred space in your bedroom. Turn to Exercise Six to learn how.

7. Do you find it difficult to focus on one task for long periods of time? Is it hard for you to concentrate?

If yes, then turn to Exercise Seven to learn how to cultivate strong attention.

8. Do you find yourself bumping into things, tripping over your own feet, and otherwise feeling clumsy?

If this is true for you, then you may benefit from increasing awareness of your personal space. Turn to Exercise Eight to learn more.

9. Do you feel closed off from the world around you? Do you feel alone or quick to mistrust people?

If so, turn to Exercise Nine to learn an easy way to cultivate trust and love.

10. Are you negatively affected by the words and opinions of others? Do you feel emotionally raw from life experiences?

If you answered yes, then learning to work with your emotions in a positive way may be of benefit. Turn to Exercise Ten to learn how.

EXERCISE ONE: SEAL YOUR SPACE

Question: Do you feel over-simulated and tense around crowds, loud noises, and bright lights?

If you answered yes, then you may need to seal your space. Sometimes your chakras and energy system are too open and life can become overwhelming. In the case of being extra sensitive to bright lights, loud noises, and chaotic crowds, your crown chakra is the one that is over-stimulated and too open. You can say the passage below when you notice these feelings. You can also say it preventatively before entering a crowded or loud area like an airport, concert, mall, or sporting event.

It can also be a useful pre-sleep ritual. Sometimes we are very open, and while we sleep we need to rest, and that openness can be distracting and get distorted while we are trying to process our subconscious emotions through dreams.

You can say the following words aloud or internally.

"I seal and protect all wormholes, portals, doorways, and openings in my physical and energetic bodies in all dimensions and inter-dimensions and all realities as needed for my highest good and the highest good of all life for all time. I own my space and only that which is of the light may enter. It is done."

EXERCISE TWO: DISCONNECT NIGHTLY

Question: Do you over identify with other people's feelings to the point where you are frequently worrying about other's emotional states at the expense of your own?

If you answered yes, then you may need to disconnect nightly. We are all empathic beings and have the ability to sense what others are feeling. Some people are very in tune with this ability and some are not.

Some of us are too empathic and we feel too much. Our hearts are wide open, which is great, but our boundaries are fuzzy and we suffer as a result. An easy way to keep this in check and minimize it is to disconnect nightly. This technique works on all of the chakras, especially the heart, which is where our empathic boundaries get tested the most. When we use the technique below we have the energetic space to share true compassion and be free of codependence.

The technique is extremely simple. At the end of each day you will just clear your heart of any unnecessary connections that are taking up your energetic bandwidth. Just say the words in the following passage aloud each night before bed. You can say them internally or whisper them quietly if needed and they will still work wonderfully. To remember you could put a note by your bed with the words written on it to remind you.

"I disconnect in all dimensions, all inter-dimensions, and all realities from everyone to whom I am connected as needed for my highest good for all time."

EXERCISE THREE: SMUDGE YOUR THIRD EYE

Question: Do you feel fuzzy and sore in your forehead as well as irritable and spacey?

If you answered yes, then you may need to smudge your third eye. Sometimes your third eye, or brow chakra, can get a gray film over it. It is like a window that needs washing. It can happen if you recently watched frightening, depressing, or violent media. Or it can happen if you were around people who were of lower vibration. It can also happen from marijuana use or being around marijuana use.

To clear it, you can smudge it with sound. You can also use sage and lavender to clear and soothe it. Gather any supplies you may have on hand. They can include: yoga or meditation chimes, wind chimes, mediation gongs, singing bowls, rattles, or lighter sounding musical instruments. You can also use lavender essential oil and rub it on your temples and forehead. And you can use a sage, lavender, and/or cedar smudge stick that you gently light on fire and wave in front of your forehead and throughout your aura all around your body.

Now sit in a relaxed state and use your instruments to create light and clear sound right in front of your forehead. If you do not have any instruments, you can use your voice! Emit a tone by singing "Om" or "Aum" in a long, higher pitched, sustained note for as long as you can. As you do this, use both hands and "waft" the energy of the sound up in front of your face and forehead. Repeat all sounds and smudges as needed, and make sure to go outside after for fresh air, and drink plenty of water.

EXERCISE FOUR: PROJECT YOUR TRUE VOICE

Question: When you speak in a group do people often not hear you or tell you to speak up?

If yes, then you may need to project your true voice.

Sometimes whether people hear your message is not only about how loudly you speak. It is just as much about how well you project your true voice. Imagine the energy of your mind and heart each flowing out of your mouth. That is the energetic essence of talking. And your throat chakra is the one that projects that message loud and clear.

A few things have to be in place for your message to be clear:

1. Your message has to be congruent with your beliefs and values. That is the heart energy flowing up to your throat.

2. You have to feel confident in your message or fake it till you make it. That is your will energy flowing up from your third chakra.

3. Your mind has to be in line up with your throat to express it. That does not mean you have to know what you are going to say, but that your mind is primed with clear energy.

That might sound like a tall order to have all of those things in line. But you can do a simple exercise to line everything up and help you project your true voice. Stand up and reach your hands up over your head and stretch. Now say aloud, "I now align all of my chakras to easily project my true voice and message with resonance, presence, and joyful authority for my highest good. It is done." Drop your arms, throw your shoulders back, and go speak up!

EXERCISE FIVE: ENGAGE YOUR ROOT VITALITY

Question: Do you feel like you are going through the motions of life but you are actually somewhere else?

If you answered yes, then you may need to reengage your root vitality. When you don't feel like you are really inhabiting your life, it can be a form of energetic disassociation. This is where part of your being is not properly seated in your energy body. This can happen for a few reasons:

1. Trauma in some form, even if small like a loud, startling noise or sad discussion with a friend.

2. Boredom and apathy. It is your job to make your life engaging and meaningful and find joy. If you don't, you may lose your sense of purpose.

3. Dissatisfaction with your life or with the structure of society.

We live in a complex world whose duality can be challenging. In the face of challenges we are charged with the task of staying positive and engaged as best as we can. Sometimes it will be easier to do than other times. Committing to experiencing joy every day is the healthiest thing you can do for your body, mind, and spirit.

You can also do the following exercise to reset your energy body, especially your root where everything begins. Stomp your feet. Next, vigorously rub your limbs and body and keep repeating the following over and over, "I am here. I am present in my body. I am (your name). I am joy." Make sure to rub your legs and feet very firmly in this process and keep going for as long and it takes to feel fully present.

EXERCISE SIX: CULTIVATING SACRED SPACE

Question: Do you suffer from nightmares or generally experience restless sleep?

Negative sleep experiences affect many people. From a spiritual perspective, when we sleep, our energy fields are loose, relaxed, and much more open than during our waking hours. There are many reasons for this but the important thing to know is that it's possible to have peaceful, restful sleep every night. The key is setting the intention to remain in your room while you sleep. We are more than just our bodies, and sometimes those with restless sleep let their energy body drift away from the physical body. This allows for deeper processing of our waking experiences but for some people the experience is too intense.

An effective way to rid yourself of this experience is twofold. First, turn your bedroom into a sacred place. Every night as you get ready for bed, light a candle next to your bed and say aloud, "I love this space. My room is my temple. I am so relaxed and comfortable here. It's so safe." Saying the words aloud trains your brain to believe them. And this belief makes it so. In truth the entire Universe is sacred; this mantra helps you agree, on a soul level, that at least your bedroom is a part of this sacredness. When you climb into bed, blow out the candle and feel grateful for the sacred space you've created.

Second, after the lights are out and you're starting to fall asleep, place one hand over your heart and one over your belly button. Inhale slowly, deeply, and visualize white light filling up your torso, just like the air you're inhaling. Hold the breath a moment and really feel the white light glowing within you. Now exhale and let your body feel like a puddle of water: formless, completely relaxed, and free. Repeat until you fall asleep. Bathing in white light in a sacred space is not only very relaxing but can also be very healing to both body and spirit.

EXERCISE SEVEN: CULTIVATE FOCUS

Question: Do you find it difficult to focus on one task for long periods of time? Is it hard for you to concentrate?

Typically a lack of focus goes hand in hand with an overactive mind. Too much mental activity causes tension in the body and scatters the energy of the third eye. And a restless body makes it difficult to concentrate.

When lack of focus is a problem, take a five-minute break from your work and do an activity that reduces mental activity. Simple breathing at your workplace, taking a relaxing walk outside, listening to mellow music—anything to calm down helps. Doing this regularly helps break the mind's grip on the body.

Step two is to practice concentrating. Find an object or simple image to stare at. Avoid using words, as they stimulate the mind. Begin by trying to stare at the object or image for a mere ten seconds without losing focus. How difficult this is for most people. If you can hold your focus for thirty minutes without breaking concentration you're a rare individual. The combination of breaking the mind's hold on the body and training the mind to focus on one thing cures the scattered mind so common in modern society.

EXERCISE EIGHT: INCREASING PRESENCE

Question: Do you find yourself bumping into things, tripping over your own feet, and otherwise feeling clumsy?

When the body and spirit are disconnected, we are not fully present in our lives. It is very important that you are here in this lifetime. The world needs you. So be fully present as much as you can, in every situation. Sometimes working with the physical body can help balance our spiritual body, too. Many martial arts schools incorporate this idea into their teachings.

Sit completely still in a comfortable position and take turns running each hand over your body, from head to toe. At each body part tell yourself, "This is my head. This is my hair. This is my cheek." And so on. Do this a few times per week to really get to know yourself. Energetically, this practice helps your spirit "agree" to be here in this place and time.

Taking the practice a step further, increase the difficulty by walking slowly through your home doing the same touching and recognition process. As you walk around, take turns running each hand over your body saying, "This is my shoulder. This is my elbow." Again, practice this a few times per week to become fully present in your life.

Finally, focus your attention on the world around you. Whenever you can, reach out and touch all the objects you encounter (probably best to skip the people around you!), identifying each one as you touch it, such as, "This is a table. This is a chair."

Increasing presence is a very physical, worldly exercise that can have very positive benefits on your spiritual practice.

EXERCISE NINE: AGREEING TO LOVE

Question: Do you feel closed off from the world around you? Do you feel alone or quick to mistrust people?

No matter what has happened in the past, right now is a brand new opportunity to love and remain open to the world. So often we carry the pains of the past into the present, creating a future we don't want. The heart chakra is the center of our being and the door to our happiness. Here is an easy exercise to cultivate love each and every moment of our lives.

No matter where you are, what you're feeling, or what you're doing, you have to breathe. Without breath there cannot be life. The lungs are very close to the heart chakra and it's easy to connect the breath with the heart physically since they occupy a similar space.

Learn to cultivate love and open your heart chakra by consciously breathing throughout your day. Each time you inhale imagine the breath is filled with white light. As the breath fills your lungs, the white light fills your heart. With practice, each inhalation can fill your heart to overflowing with love and joy, carried along by the white light. Every time you exhale let everything else leave your being: fear, anger, attachment, resentment, revenge, worry, loss, lack, the past, mistakes—any of those things that really have no bearing on your present. In every situation, positive or negative, inhale the white light of love and exhale everything else. The white light may bring a spontaneous smile to your lips during any life experience. Mindful, heart-centered breathing opens the heart chakra, keeps us present in each moment, and helps us focus on the positive things in our lives.

EXERCISE TEN: CULTIVATING SELF-WORTH

Question: Are you negatively affected by the words and opinions of others?

If you are sensitive to energy, it can be difficult to not take on other people's thoughts, feelings, and opinions, all of which emanate from their energy fields out into the world around them. Sensitive people pick up this energy and can easily let these external influences outweigh their own beliefs. So how can you step this from happening?

Previous exercises have focused on cultivating presence, and being present to your own self will help reduce these unwanted influences, but ultimately being susceptible to other's opinions or willpower has to do with the second chakra. There are several ways to strengthen the second chakra. Physically, the yoga practice called Nakra-Kriya (Crocodile Cleansing) works each vertebrae using controlled breathing to heal the second chakra. Internally, daily mantras are a great way to retrain your personal beliefs about yourself. Whenever you feel negatively affected by others, say to yourself, "I am amazing. I know what I believe. I love myself." Close your eyes and say, "I cannot control others; I can only control myself. And I choose to love myself."

BIBLIOGRAPHY

For more information about chakras, we invite you to explore all of the wonderful resources listed below. From ancient texts to modern perspectives on the subject, you will find a wide array of opinions about chakras, the human energy field, and energy healing.

Avalon, Arthur. *The Serpent Power: The Secrets of Tantric & Shaktic Yoga.* Dover Publications, Inc.: New York, NY, 1974.

Beckman, Howard. *Mantras, Yantras & Fabulous Gems: The Healing Secrets of the Ancient Vedas.* Balaji Publishing Co., 1996.

Chia, Mantak. *Awaken Healing Energy Through the Tao: The Taoist Secret of Circulating Internal Power.* Aurora Press: Santa Fe, NM, 1983.

Dale, Cyndi. *The Subtle Body: An Encyclopedia of Your Energetic Anatomy.* Boulder, CO: Sounds True, 2009.

Feuerstein, Georg. *Tantra: The Path of Ecstasy.* Shambhala Publications: Boston & London, 1998.

Goswami, Shyam. *Layayoga: The Definitive Guide to the Chakras and Kundalini.* Inner Traditions: Rochester, VT, 1999.

Judith, Anodea. *Wheels of Life.* Woodbury, MN: Llewellyn Publications, 2015.

Maupin, Kathy C. and Newcomb, Brett. *The Secret Female Hormone: How Testosterone Replacement Therapy Can Change Your Life.* Hay House: Carlsbad, CA, 2014.

Mercree, Amy. *The Spiritual Girl's Guide to Dating: Your Enlightened Path to Love, Sex and Soul Mates.* Adams Media: Avon, MA, 2012.

Mercree, Chad. *The Way of the Psychic Heart: Developing Your Spiritual Gifts in the Everyday World*. Llewellyn Publications: Woodbury, MN, 2014.

Ranganathananda, Swami. *The Message of the Upanishads*. Chowpatty: Mumbai, India, 1971.

Rinpoche, Tenzin Wangyal. *Awakening the Sacred Body*. New York: Hay House, 2011.

Sarno, John E. *Healing Back Pain*. Warner Books: New York, NY, 1991.

Vittii, Alisa. *Woman Code: Perfect Your Cycle, Amplify Your Fertility, Super Charge Your Sex Drive, and Become a Power Source*. Harper One: New York, NY, 2013.

ENDNOTES
Chapter Five

"As an endocrine gland it secretes the hormones insulin and glucagon to control blood sugar levels." The Mayo Clinic. [http://www.mayoclinic.org/diseases-conditions/hypoglycemia/basics/causes/con-20021103]

"Mind/body remedies to help with both of these include: tai chi, yoga, and Ayurveda (a Hindu system of medicine, which is based on the idea of balance in all bodily systems and proper diet, herbal treatments, and yogic breathing.)" Chopra Centered Lifestyle. [http://www.chopra.com/ccl/a-mind-body-approach-to-diabetes]

Chapter Six

"Before puberty your thymus produces lots of thymosin, a hormone that helps your body produce T-cells which play a vital role in immunity for your whole lifetime." Endocrine Web. [http://www.endocrineweb.com/endocrinology/overview-thymus]

ACKNOWLEDGMENTS

The authors would like to thank Lisa Hagan for being a marvelous agent and steadfast champion of our work. We would also like to thank Kate Zimmermann for her valuable assistance and for allowing us to share this book with the world. We are also grateful to our loving and supportive families who cheer on our literary adventures. Amy would like to thank Laurie Levity Laughing Star for her support in Amy's early explorations in the world of chakras.

ABOUT THE AUTHORS

AMY LEIGH MERCREE'S motto is "Live joy. Be kind. Love unconditionally." She counsels women and men in the underrated art of self-love to create happier lives. Amy is an author, media personality, and expert dating, relationship, and wellness coach, as well as a medical intuitive. Mercree speaks internationally, focusing on kindness, joy, and wellness. She is also a screenwriter and film producer.

Mercree is the author of *The Spiritual Girl's Guide to Dating: Your Enlightened Path to Love, Sex, and Soul Mates* and the upcoming book *Joyful Living: 101 Ways to Transform Your Spirit and Revitalize Your Life.*

Check out AmyLeighMercree.com for articles, picture quotes, and quizzes. Mercree is fast becoming one of the most quoted women on the Web. See what all the buzz is about at @AmyLeighMercree on Twitter.

CHAD MERCREE is the author of *The Way of the Psychic Heart* and *A Little Bit of Buddha* and has written and lectured on botanical and metaphysical subjects for most of his adult life. His has studied Hatha and Kundalini Yoga for many years, and he's also a student of Dzogchen Buddhism, an offshoot of Tantric Buddhism. Chad leads workshops throughout the United States on meditation, spiritual awakening, and connecting spiritually and scientifically to the natural world around us. He lives in Naples, FL.

INDEX